Lice

Kris Hirschmann

**KIDHAVEN
PRESS**™

THOMSON

GALE

San Diego • Detroit • New York • San Francisco • Cleveland
New Haven, Conn. • Waterville, Maine • London • Munich

THOMSON
™
GALE

© 2004 by KidHaven Press. KidHaven Press is an imprint of The Gale Group, Inc.,
a division of Thomson Learning, Inc.

KidHaven™ and Thomson Learning™ are trademarks used herein under license.

For more information, contact
KidHaven Press
27500 Drake Rd.
Farmington Hills, MI 48331-3535
Or you can visit our Internet site at http://www.gale.com

LIBRARY OF CONGRESS CATALOGING-IN-PUBLICATION DATA

Hirschmann, Kris, 1967-
  Lice / by Kris Hirschmann.
    v. cm. — (Parasites)
  Includes bibliographical references (p.) and index.
  Contents: Human-loving parasites—Infestation—Lice in action—The fight against lice.
    ISBN 0-7377-1784-X (hardback : alk. paper)
    1. Lice—Juvenile literature. 2. Lice as carriers of
  disease—Juvenile literature. [1. Lice.] I. Title. II. Series.
    RA641.L6H55 2004
    614.4'324—dc22

2003012157

Printed in China

CONTENTS

CHAPTER 1

Human-Loving Parasites

Everyone's head feels itchy sometimes. Usually this means nothing. Sometimes, however, it signals a problem. Itchiness may mean that a person carries lice—tiny creatures that **infest** the bodies of birds and mammals, including humans.

Lice are **parasites**, which means they live and feed on other animals. These animals are called **hosts**. A **louse** survives by drinking the blood or bodily fluids of its host.

What Are Lice?

Lice are insects. There are more than three thousand different species of these creatures. Nearly all species are tiny, measuring an eighth of an inch or

Lice are parasites that drink the blood of other animals, including humans.

Lice have six legs and two antennae, and are usually the same color as their hosts.

less from end to end. All lice have six legs ending in claws, two **antennae**, and hard-shelled bodies. They are usually the same color as the animals they infest.

There are two main types of lice: chewing lice and sucking lice. Chewing lice infest birds and mammals. They gnaw on the skin of their hosts to get blood and tissue fluids. Sucking lice infest only mammals. They eat by piercing the host's skin with mouthparts called **stylets**, then slurping the flowing blood.

Lice must eat constantly to survive. They quickly die of starvation if they are separated from their hosts. For this reason lice are rarely seen on their own. Usually they are found on or very near their host animals.

Human Lice

Only three species of lice infest humans. These species are called body lice, head lice, and crab lice. All of these creatures are sucking lice that drink blood to survive.

Body lice and head lice look almost identical. Both species have long bodies, slender legs, and delicate claws. The only real difference between these insects is their living habits. Body lice are found below the neck. They often crawl off the body into the seams of clothing. Head lice live only on the head, especially behind the ears and at the hairline of the neck. They seldom leave their host.

Crab lice look very different from body and head lice. Their bodies are thicker and shorter. They have heavy, crablike claws at the ends of their legs. Crab lice usually infest pubic hair, but sometimes they spread to armpits and other areas where the hair is thick and coarse.

How Lice Spread

Lice cannot hop or fly. They must crawl from one victim to the next. Therefore most infestations happen when a person touches someone who carries lice. People can also get lice if they use the personal objects of an infested person. Why? Lice sometimes fall or crawl onto clothing, hair brushes, ribbons, bedding, stuffed animals, or other things that touch the human body. When an uninfested person uses these things, the lice crawl right onto the new host.

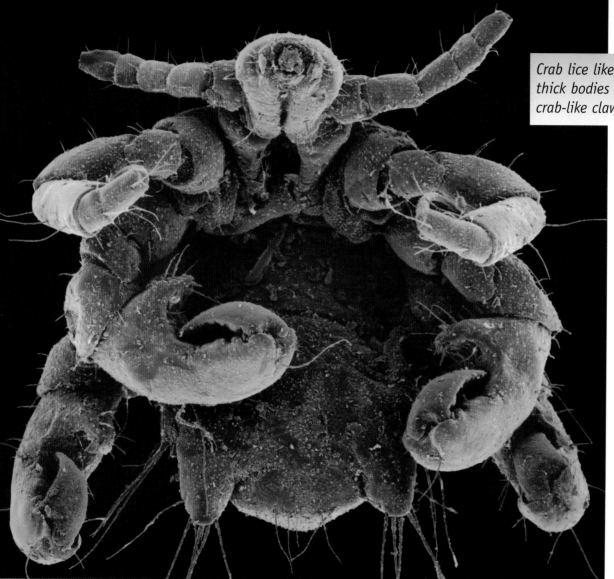

Crab lice like this one have thick bodies and large, crab-like claws.

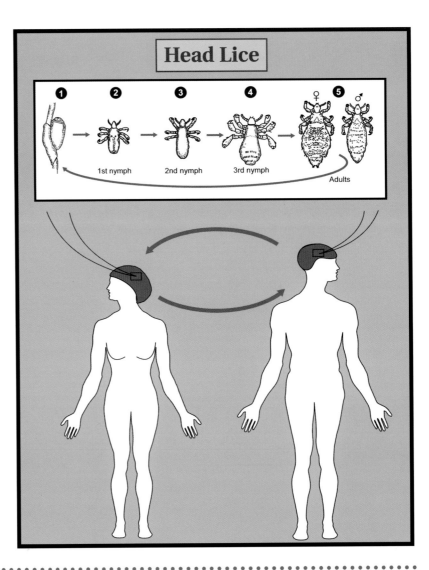

This chart shows the various stages of the head louse life cycle, from egg (above left) to adult (above right).

Anyone Can Get Lice

Some people think lice are a sign of poor **hygiene**. This is true of body lice, which thrive in dirty, crowded conditions. Head and crab lice, on the other hand, will happily infest even the cleanest person. In fact, head lice might even like cleaner people better. So lice should not be a source of shame. People must realize that anyone can become a home for these creepy-crawly parasites.

Infestation

It does not take much to start a lice problem. A female louse can lay dozens of eggs on a host within a couple of days. Soon these eggs hatch into a horde of bloodsucking babies. A full-blown infestation has begun.

The Lice Feed

Lice begin eating as soon as they arrive on a human host. To feed, a louse pushes three sharp mouthparts called stylets out of its head. It uses these stylets to scratch the skin and make the host bleed. The louse then sucks up the flowing blood. It uses the claws at the ends of its legs to cling to strands of

Lice use sharp mouthparts called stylets to make their hosts bleed.

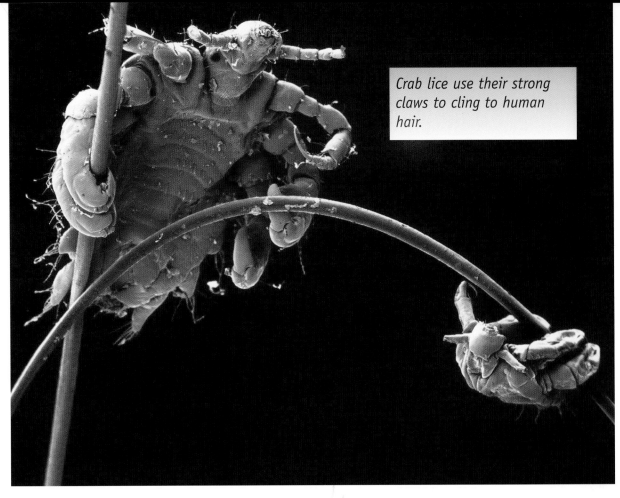

Crab lice use their strong claws to cling to human hair.

hair as it eats. This keeps the parasite from being shaken loose before it finishes its meal.

As a louse feeds it injects a special saliva into the host that keeps blood from clotting. The saliva often causes a skin reaction. This is the reason lice make their victims so itchy. Lice take several blood meals each day, so an infested person soon bears dozens or even hundreds of uncomfortable bites.

Laying Eggs

Drinking blood gives lice the strength they need to reproduce. Males and females mate while on the host. Females then lay oval eggs, which are called **nits**. Nits are grayish or white in color. They are just one-thirtieth of an inch long—about the size of a period at the end of a sentence. These tiny eggs need warmth to develop. The female places them where they will get lots of heat from the host's body. Head lice and crab lice glue their nits to the base of hair strands close to the host's skin. Body lice cement their nits to clothing fibers and seams.

Once a female begins laying nits, she never stops. She deposits new nits every day for the rest of her life. Crab lice produce about thirty nits in their lifetimes. Head lice produce between fifty and one hundred nits, and body lice can lay as many as three hundred nits before they die.

From Nymph to Adult

It takes seven to ten days for a nit to hatch. The newly hatched louse is called a **nymph**. Nymphs look a lot like adult lice, but they are much smaller, and their bodies are colorless.

Nymphs are born hungry. As soon as these creatures hatch, they begin to eat. A nymph gorges itself on its host's blood six or seven times a day. This rich diet makes the nymph strong and helps it to grow. Before long the parasite is ready to **molt**. This means it sheds its outer covering and takes on a new and bigger shape.

A nymph molts three times before it becomes an adult. The entire process takes just one to two weeks. After the molts are complete, the louse will live about a month as an adult. During this period the louse will spend its time drinking blood, mating, and laying a new generation of nits.

Crawling with Lice

Lice do not go away on their own. If an infestation is not stopped, it will grow and grow. A person with a

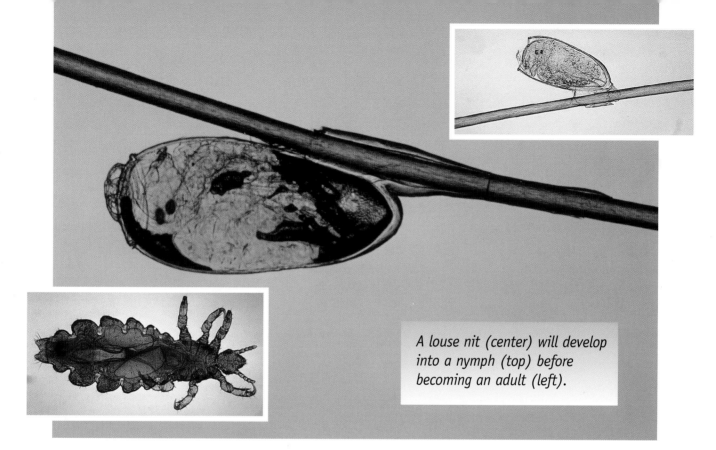

A louse nit (center) will develop into a nymph (top) before becoming an adult (left).

bad head-lice problem may carry hundreds of nits, nymphs, and lice. In extreme cases lice may even invade the eyebrows and eyelashes as they run out of room on the head. These parasites may be small, but they send big shivers of disgust through the people who become their victims.

Lice in Action

L ice are the most common human parasites in the world today. They were an even bigger problem in earlier ages, when most people lived in crowded and unclean conditions. In fact lice have been infesting people since the beginning of recorded history.

Head Lice

Head lice are not as common today as they once were. However there are still plenty of these creatures around, and they can show up without warning in any home on Earth.

One mother learned this lesson when she noticed her son scratching his head. She parted the boy's hair and peeked at his scalp. Sure enough the boy was crawling with lice. The mother immediately washed her son's hair with a special lice-killing shampoo and combed it to remove the bugs. She changed the boy's sheets, washed his clothes, and

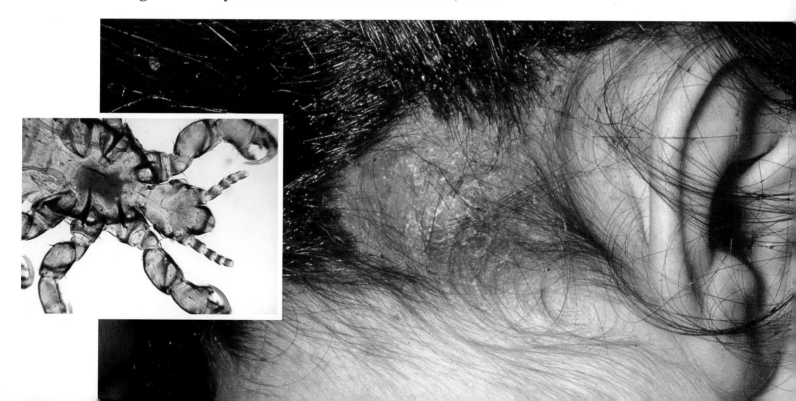

Lice are the most common human parasites. Here, a louse bite has become infected.

sealed all his personal things in plastic bags. But nothing worked. Every time the mother checked her son's head, the lice were back. Even worse, the boy passed the lice to his classmates at school. The children infested and reinfested each other for more than two months before all the parents, working together, finally killed the last louse.

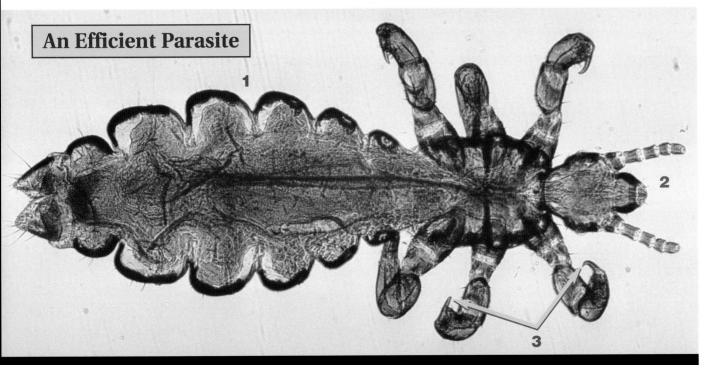

An Efficient Parasite

1 The louse's hard shell is the same color as the host and helps the louse to hide easily.

2 Mouthparts called stylets are used to pierce the host's skin and slurp up the flowing blood.

3 Sharp claws help the louse attach to hair or clothing while feeding or laying eggs.

This mother's experience was not unusual. Each year head lice infest millions of American children. It takes a lot of time, effort, and money to stop these infestations.

Body Lice

Infestations are even harder to stop in close quarters, such as battle trenches. During World War I American soldiers were plagued by body lice. One new soldier described the sight that greeted him when he first reported for duty: "We got a shock when the other soldiers in the hut took their shirts off. . . . They were catching lice. The men were killing them between their nails. . . . We soon found out that this took the better part of an hour daily. Each day brought a new batch; as fast as you killed them, others took their place." [1]

Another soldier described his clothing: "[Lice] lay in the seams of trousers, in the deep furrows of long thick woolly pants. . . . A lighted candle applied where they were thickest made them pop like Chinese crackers. After a session of this, my face would be covered with small blood spots from extra

big fellows which had popped too vigorously [made a large noise burst]."[2]

Lice and Disease

Body lice are not just uncomfortable. They also carry diseases. The worst louse-borne disease is called **typhus**. Typhus victims experience high fever, muscle and joint pain, headaches, and rashes. Many patients become **delirious**, and more than half die.

A severe typhus outbreak struck Poland during World War II. At the epidemic's peak the death rate reached five thousand people per month. A survivor described the horrifying situation: "There was no way of burying those who died of typhus fast enough. . . . The dead were stripped of their clothes and were put outside on the pavements wrapped in paper. They often waited there for days until Council vehicles came to collect them and take them away to mass graves in the cemetery."[3]

Even today typhus outbreaks are common in some parts of the world. But they are nearly unknown in places where sanitation is good. Cleanliness helps people to avoid body lice and the dangerous diseases they carry.

CHAPTER 4

The Fight Against Lice

Wherever people go, lice are sure to follow. These creatures are so common that it is impossible to get rid of them. And once lice infest a person's head or body, they can be very hard to destroy.

Persistent Parasites

Lice infestations are hard to stop for many reasons. One reason is that these parasites are small and difficult to see. Even if lice *are* seen, they can crawl away very quickly. Lice also hate light so they immediately burrow deeper into a person's hair or clothing when they are uncovered. Between their speed and their "disappearing" habits, lice are not easy to catch.

Another problem is that lice cling tightly to a host's hair with their clawed legs. This makes the parasites hard to remove. Nits, too, are firmly

A head louse hides from the light of day at the base of a human hair.

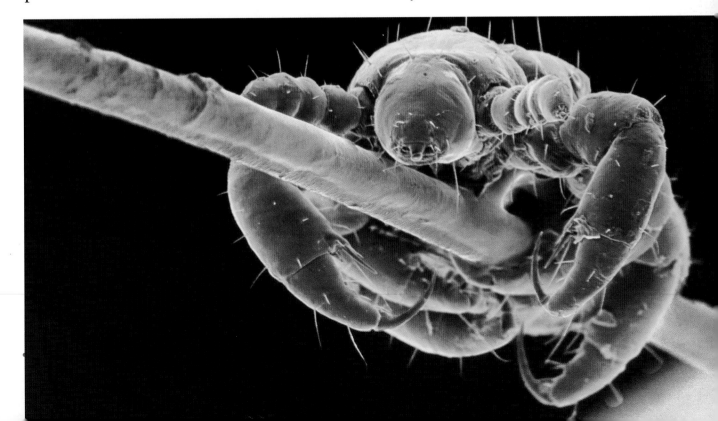

attached. They are glued so tightly to hair shafts that they cannot be shaken loose by shampooing or simple combing. To remove nits a person must either use a special fine-toothed comb, or find the nits and pull them off one by one. If a single nit is missed, a new infestation may occur.

Lice infestations are difficult to control. Here, a louse hangs between two hairs.

Poisoning Lice

Many insects can be controlled with chemical sprays. But this does not work with lice. Since these creatures live only on animal hosts, spraying rooms or yards does no good at all. Head lice can, however, be killed with shampoos that contain **pesticides** (chemicals that are deadly to insects). Permethrin, pyrethrin, and malathion are a few of the pesticides that lice victims apply to their heads. These shampoos kill only lice, not nits, so they must be used again after any nits have hatched.

Stopping the Spread

Because lice are so hard to kill, it is best to stop them from spreading in the first place. In the fight against body lice, cleanliness is the best weapon. Typhus and other louse-borne diseases are very rare in developed countries. And even if people do get sick, they can usually be cured with modern health care and drugs.

There is also a **vaccine** that prevents typhus. A vaccinated person will not become sick even if he or she is bitten by a disease-carrying louse. However,

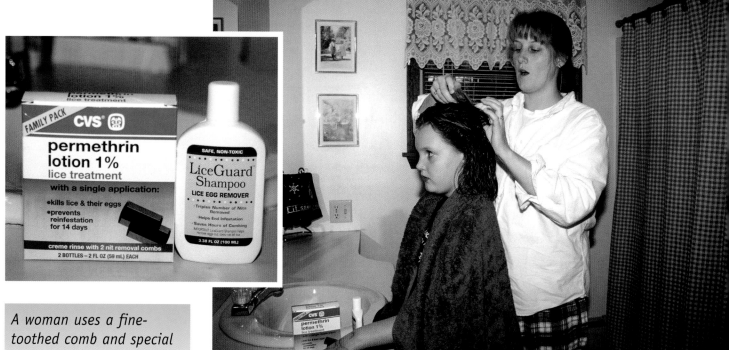

A woman uses a fine-toothed comb and special shampoo (inset) to remove lice from her daughter's hair.

this vaccine is no longer made in the United States. So people who travel to countries where typhus is common must be careful to avoid infested areas.

No matter how careful people are, however, they may still become infested with lice. These parasites have lived on humans for thousands upon thousands of years, and they are not about to stop now. As long as humans live on Earth, they will continue to be plagued by lice.

Chapter 3: Lice in Action

1. Quoted in *Spartacus Educational,* "Lice." www.spartacus.schoolnet.co.uk.

2. George Coppard, *With a Machine Gun to Cambrai.* New York: Orion, 1999. Quoted in *Spartacus Educational.*

3. Wladyslaw Szpilman, *The Pianist: The Extraordinary True Story of One Man's Survival in Warsaw, 1939–45.* New York: Picador USA, 1999. www.barnesandnoble.com.

GLOSSARY

antennae: Sensory organs on a louse's head.

delirious: Not in control of one's mind. Delirious patients may be confused, have trouble speaking, or see things that are not really there.

host: A plant or animal whose body provides shelter or food for a parasite.

hygiene: Personal cleanliness.

infest: To live in or on as a parasite.

louse: The singular form of "lice."

molt: To shed the outer covering of the body.

nit: A louse egg.

nymph: The first body stage in the louse's life cycle.

parasite: A creature that lives on or feeds from another living organism.

pesticide: A chemical that is deadly to insects.

stylets: The three sharp mouthparts of sucking lice.

typhus: A deadly disease that is carried by human-body lice.

vaccine: A substance that, when taken into the body, prevents a disease.

Books

Howard and Margery Facklam, *Parasites*. New York: Twenty-First Century, 1994. Read about bloodsucking parasites, invasive worms, harmful bacteria, and more in this book.

Jamie Gilson, *Itchy Richard*. New York: Clarion, 1991. This fiction book is about a boy who is afraid he might have lice.

Allison Lassieur, *Head Lice*. New York: Franklin Watts, 2000. Read more about head lice and how to get rid of them.

Website

Head Games (www.headlice.org). Includes lice games, word searches, quizzes, and more. A fun way to learn about head lice.

INDEX

appearance, 7

blood, 4, 14–15
body lice
  appearance of, 7–8
  disease and, 22–23
  hygiene and, 11
  infestations of,
    21–22
  nits of, 15

chewing lice, 7
claws, 13–14, 25
crab lice
  appearance of, 8
  hygiene and, 11
  nits of, 15

diseases, 22–23

eggs. *See* nits

feeding, 12–15

head lice
  appearance of, 7–8
  hygiene and, 11
  infestations of, 19–21
  nits of, 15
hosts, 4, 7
human lice species, 7
hygiene, 11, 23

infestations, 16–17
  of body lice, 21–22
  of head lice, 19–21
  persistence of, 24–26
  spreading of, 8, 11

malathion, 27
molting, 16

nits, 15–16
  attachment of, 25

described, 15–16
  pesticides and, 27
nymphs, 16

parasites, 4
permethrin, 27
pesticides, 27
pyrethrin, 27

saliva, 14–15
shampoo, 27
size, 5, 7
species, 5
stylets, 7, 13
sucking lice, 7

typhus, 23, 27–28

vaccines, 27–28

World War I, 21–22